Public Speaking Success

101 Proven Steps to Successful Speeches, Pitches & Presentations

Andy O'Sullivan

Beatrice

To whom I owe it all

LEGAL NOTICES

The information presented herein represents the view of the author as of the date of publication. Because of the rate with which conditions change, the author's reserve the right to alter and update his opinion based on the new conditions. This book is for informational purposes only. While every attempt has been made to verify the information provided in this book, neither the authors nor their affiliates/partners assume any responsibility for errors, inaccuracies or omissions. Any slights of people or organizations are unintentional. If advice concerning legal, financial or any other real estate related matters is needed, the services of a fully qualified professional should be sought. This book is not intended for use as a source of legal or accounting advice.

STATEMENT OF EARNINGS/DISCLAIMER. Every effort has been made to accurately represent this product and its potential. Examples in these materials are not to be interpreted as a promise or guarantee of earnings. Earning potential is entirely dependent on the person using our product, ideas and techniques. We do not purport this as a "get rich scheme."

Your level of success in attaining the results claimed in our materials depends on the time you devote to the program, ideas and techniques mentioned, your finances, knowledge and various skills. Since these factors differ according to individuals, we cannot guarantee your success or income level. Nor are we responsible for any of your actions.

Materials in our product and our website may contain information that includes or is based upon forward-looking statements. Forward-looking statements give our expectations or forecasts of future events. You can identify these statements by the fact that they do not relate strictly to historical or current facts. They use words such as "anticipate," "estimate," "expect," "project," "intend," "plan," "believe," and other words and terms of similar meaning in connection with a description of potential earnings or financial performance.

ALL RIGHTS RESERVED. No part of this book may be reproduced or transmitted in any form whatsoever, electronic, or mechanical, including photocopying, recording, or by any informational storage or retrieval without the expressed written consent of the authors.

© Andy O'Sullivan

If you do not wish to be bound by the above, you may return this book to the publisher for a full refund.

TABLE OF CONTENTS

Introduction	Who is Andy O'Sullivan Why You Will Want to Listen. How He Will Save You Pain.	13
CHAPTER 1	**Eliminating Anxiety**	33
1	Some Speakers Are So Confident	34
2	Seeing the Source	36
3	Taking Action	37
4	Relieving the Anxiety	39
5	Staying Calm	40
6	Seeking Support	42
7	Presentation Posture	43
8	Resisting Any Changes	44
9	Notice Your Audience	45
CHAPTER 2	**Imperative Information**	47
10	Discover Your Purpose	48
11	One Question to Ask	49
12	Timing Their Interest	50
13	Know Who Will Be There	51
14	Assessing the Resources	52
15	Advance Questions	53
16	Who it is Really About	55

CHAPTER 3	Investigating Ideas	57
17	Creativity of Your Hand	58
18	What is The Idea?	59
19	Conveying Your	61
20	Trimming Your List	63
21	Building the Detail	64
22	Creating a Connection	65
23	Exposing Concerns	66
24	Time to Browse	67

CHAPTER 4	Structuring Your Speech	69
25	Pique Their Interest	70
26	Capturing Attention	71
27	Seeing the Sound	72
28	Advantages of Listening	73
29	Getting Personal	74
30	A Question to Contemplate	75
31	Source of a Story	76
32	Positive Endings	77
33	Discarding Details	78
34	Paring the Points	79
35	Aiding Recollection	80
36	Gathering the Points	81
37	Captivating Comments	82
38	Confessing Your Concerns	84

CHAPTER 5	**Sharpening Your Speaking Skills**	87
39	Audience Connections	88
40	Making it Easy	89
41	Slowing the Speech	90
42	Benefiting from Knowledge	91
43	Include it All	93

CHAPTER 6	**PowerPoint Perfection**	95
44	Looking the Best	96
45	Reducing the Files	97
46	Explain and Expand	98
47	Contacting the Speaker	100
48	Missing Mistakes	103
49	Timing Your Slides	104
50	Showing Slides Online	105
51	Pressing the Right Buttons	107

CHAPTER 7	**Presenting Your Presentation**	109
52	Moving to Attention	110
53	Adding Emphasis	112
54	Backwards and Forwards	114
55	A Suitable Spot	116
56	Stepping Off the Stag	118

CHAPTER 8	Confidently Answering Questions	121
57	Thinking of Your Own Questions	122
58	Who Will Be the Leader?	124
59	Express a Preference	125
60	Question to Ask	126
61	Choosing Your Question	128
62	Valuing the Questions	129
63	Honesty is The Best Policy	130
64	Being Impolite	131
65	Serving Your Best	132
66	Achieving Focus	133
67	Encouraging Participation	134

CHAPTER 9	Visual Communication	137
68	Creating a Natural Connection	138
69	Naturally Gesturing	140
70	Showing Your Hand	142
71	Controlling Your Confidence	143

CHAPTER 10	Recording and Reviewing	145
72	Finding Your Favourites	146
73	Repetitive Gestures	147
74	Seeing a Straight Stance	148

CHAPTER 11 Success Planning — 149
- 75 Arranging Your Resources — 150
- 76 Planning a Positive Impression — 151
- 77 Dressing to Impress — 153
- 78 Contrasting Clothes — 154
- 79 Awareness of Announcements — 155
- 80 Preparing for Probability — 156

CHAPTER 12 Showing Up and Stepping Up — 157
- 81 Need to Know? — 158
- 82 Every Little Thing Matters — 159
- 83 Checking the Connection — 160
- 84 Amplified for Audio — 161
- 85 Sidestep the Buzz — 162
- 86 Promptly Preparing — 163
- 87 Seeing the Speaker — 164
- 88 Eradicating Diversions — 165
- 89 Protruding Pockets — 166
- 90 Your Crucial Sentences — 167

CHAPTER 13	Presentation Perfection	169
91	Sticking to It	170
92	Source of Stress	171
93	Talking to the Wall	172
94	Short Summary	173
95	Seeing the Signs	174
96	Releasing Their Concerns	175
97	Private Conversation	177
98	Keeping Your Credibility	178
99	Pausing for Confidence	179
100	Sharing the Sentiment	181
101	Significant Slip?	182

About Andy O'Sullivan   183

Acknowledgements   187

References   191

Bibliography   193

Introduction

INTRODUCTION

Who is Andy O'Sullivan… and How You Can Now Benefit From All His Pain, Panic and Practice

You may have noticed that whenever there are young children around, they are always happy to play and perform in public.

They are happy to dance, sing, or play instruments in front of family, friends and neighbours.

They will happily do all these things without any fears or worries about getting embarrassed, looking silly or even being judged.

Then something happens to change us.

Introduction

Something happens that causes us to change the way we see ourselves. This change now makes us worry about what others will think about us.

This change occurs somewhere between childhood and adulthood. It is a change that steals away all the natural confidence we all had when we were born and enjoyed throughout those early years of life.

Rather than feeling happy, relaxed and even excited to perform in front of others, grabbing every opportunity we could ever find, we are now fearful when standing and speaking.

These feelings of fear, panic and pending doom take over immediately we are faced with the ordeal of having to speak in public.

Just the thought of standing and speaking at a meeting that may be weeks away is enough to fill our bodies with all those feelings of dread and fear.

If the idea of speaking in public now fills us with all these unpleasant feelings, I am sure having to sing or dance in front of other people would for many now be a whole lot worse!

What Changed?

So what has happened to change things for us?

What is it that has changed us from feeling happy and confident when performing to now having all those negative feelings fill our bodies whenever we are in these situations?

You may have heard of the 'fight or flight response' we have whenever we are placed in a stressful situation, like delivering a pitch.

While this is likely to have played a part in my fear of public speaking, there was another factor that affected how I felt about standing in front of large groups with everyone looking at me.

A big part of my fear and, dare I even say, hatred of speaking in public was all down to my early education.

As I now look back, it is a pity that neither of the schools that I attended ever had a programme where they would help us to develop our communication skills and confidence.

These are the skills so critical to achieving success throughout our professional lives.

If anything, the way the schools operated was totally the opposite.

Punishment and Embarrassment

At my schools, public speaking was used as a punishment by many of my teachers.

If the teachers felt you or the class were misbehaving in any way, they would force us to read either our work or, even worse, from a textbook to the whole class.

As a young child, struggling to read in front of the class of thirty or so other children, I would naturally stumble or hesitate over some of the words.

This situation was more likely to occur if the words were new to me or in another language that I was learning at the time.

What was the result?

The whole class would immediately erupt into laughter, sometimes even pointing and making unpleasant comments.

I would be left standing there in front of the entire class feeling embarrassed, upset and very much alone.

Placing a child in this position was not a way to help build their confidence and self-esteem during those early formative years.

Introduction

It was not the fault of all the other children in my class in the way they behaved towards me.

Nor was it mine when I did the same during their public reading sessions as they too stumbled over their words, sometimes silently standing there, red with embarrassment.

Haunting Memories

Throughout my school days, speaking or reading in public therefore became an experience to be feared and one to avoid at all costs.

When I meet up with some of my old school friends, we are still haunted by the experiences of those public reading punishments, decades later.

Does this make my fear of public speaking the fault of my teachers?

They were the ones who made the idea of speaking in public something to be feared, making us individually stand up in front of the whole class and read to everyone.

I used to think it was.

Reflecting to Forgive

Now, on reflection, I feel they would never genuinely do anything if they knew the effect it would have on us.

Little did they know the effect these regular humiliations would have on both my classmates and me as we grew up and became adults.

In many of the private schools here in the UK and other education systems around the world, they actively encourage and support public speaking.

Schools will have debating clubs and inter-school contests all aimed at developing their students' speaking skills.

Training in how to communicate and confidently speak in public is something I would love to see in every school, worldwide.

Adulthood

As a young adult, I would always hate being the centre of attention and therefore would work to ensure it was avoided at all costs.

This hatred had an immense effect on both my career and even whenever I was out socialising.

Many years ago, after starting a trainee job at a new company, I was always invited out for some after work drinks on Fridays.

In the bar with my new colleagues, we would often have other people from the department in which we worked join us.

These were people who I had never met or had only had a very brief conversation with.

Vividly I recall how the thought of having to stand there in front of everyone, with them all looking at me, totally scared me as I asked the straightforward question of what drink they would like.

Standing in front of the group, with them all staring at me, was public speaking and I hated it!

It was something that I wanted to avoid at all costs, so came up with an ingenious plan.

Whenever it came to buying a round of drinks (which I was delighted to do), I would always ask one of my close colleagues to get the drinks in and I would give them the money.

Easy!

On reflection, as I was never seen to buy any drinks, all the other people who joined us for those Friday drinks probably perceived me as being very tight with money.

My colleagues, on the other hand, must have been seen to be very generous.

Either way, getting my colleagues to take the orders and buy the drinks never helped me to overcome my fear of speaking in public.

Avoidance

Throughout my career, I carried on taking every opportunity possible to avoid being in the same situation of speaking in public.

This avoidance would often mean not participating in meetings where there were many attendees or feeling unable to voice my opinion to any proposals presented, even when I was against them.

Career Block

The lack of confidence to speak in public would affect my career as changing jobs and attending the inevitable interviews were all part of the process.

It would entail having to sit in the interview with people asking lots of questions while looking at me.

This was scary!

If an interview with one or two people scared me, the idea of a panel type process was entirely out of the question.

The thought of facing an interview panel scared me so much, I would avoid applying for any jobs where this was a known part of the process.

While trying to secure what I felt would be my ideal job, there could be other unexpected hurdles.

Once, having cruised through the interview process for what I felt was the perfect job, I hit a huge hurdle.

The company decided all of the shortlisted candidates would need to deliver a 3 to 5 minute presentation to the members of the department in which they would work if successful in their application.

I could not think of anything worse and immediately withdrew my application for the role.

Facing one or two people in an interview was a terrifying thought for me. The idea of a public presentation was just too much.

Achieving My Potential

It was some years later while working for an international bank that my fears of speaking up in public came to a head.

My management always perceived me to be a 'good worker', which I was, but something was missing. I wanted more.

Being ambitious, I naturally wanted to have more success in my career, to get promoted, to have a more substantial salary.

Continually, I kept seeing newer and less experienced colleagues climbing the corporate career ladder ahead of me.

What was it that they were doing to get this success?

Speaking and Saying Nothing New

These colleagues were the ones who were always actively participating in meetings.

You would find that they would always have an opinion to share in meetings, especially when senior management were present.

Introduction

On most occasions, the views and ideas they shared were not even their own!

Sometimes all they would do is just repeat and rephrase what somebody else in the meeting had already stated.

Continually, these were the same people the management liked.

While I stayed in exactly the same role, never moving up the corporate career ladder, my colleagues who spoke up became the people who always got noticed, promoted and rewarded.

It became abundantly clear to me that, no matter how hard you work, no matter what hours you are putting in, working evenings and weekends, to stand any chance of getting success, you have to be seen and heard.

That is when it dawned on me! I had to improve my communication skills.

The Journey

As I started out on what was for me a long and tough journey to becoming a more confident public speaker and presenter, I was continually on the lookout for that 'magic pill'.

The one simple step or strategy that would quickly allow me always to feel confident whenever I needed to speak in public.

In my search for this 'magic pill', I started attending countless courses, workshops and seminars and reading all the books on public speaking that I could find.

There were also all of the online courses, articles and videos which I spent many, many hours devouring over my evenings and weekends.

You can find countless tips, tools and techniques on the internet.

Introduction

They all seem to promise they will help us become better speakers, to have more confidence, to deal better with all those surprise speaking situations.

To the uninitiated, there is also a lot of, dare I say, 'rubbish' that is said about public speaking.

At best it is worthless, while at the worst, it will damage your confidence and along with it any chance you have of achieving success.

After wasting much time and money being given a false belief of instant confidence, having been taught techniques that are ridiculous, I came to what is an obvious conclusion.

There is no 'magic pill'.

Not one simple technique will give you the confidence and skills to allow you to deal with an awkward question, argumentative client or cope when things go terribly wrong.

It was after this realisation that I began what was to become a long and, at times, painful journey of growth.

A journey that would take me from being filled with panic, days before I was due to deliver a pitch or presentation.

Where I would spend days rehearsing my every word, only to deliver pitches and presentations that were seen as a 'major embarrassment'.

Not my words.

Those were the words of my manager at the time.

The very person that I had always been hoping to impress by speaking in public.

Not A Natural

You can probably guess, even as an adult, I was not a 'natural' public speaker, yet today that is precisely what everyone perceives me as being.

Introduction

When people see me regularly delivering perfect pitches or presentations in large auditoriums, they tell me afterwards that I am a 'natural' and how easy it is for 'people like me'.

Those who see me delivering confident speeches and presentations, even off-the-cuff, have not witnessed or seen the pain and panic that got me into the position where I am today, regularly winning awards and recognition for all my continual achievements.

The journey I have been through over all these years was not pleasant or enjoyable, yet it has taught me a tremendous amount.

It has taught me what works, and most importantly what does not.

It is all this first-hand knowledge and experience that is now available for you in this book.

Lucky you!

You now get the benefit of all the pain, stress and upset that I went through, which will now ensure you become confident and competent as you now successfully create and deliver winning speeches, presentations and pitches with the tips in this book.

Enjoy the journey....

I will be here every step of the way.

Andy O'Sullivan
andy@academyofpublicspeakers.com
www.academyofpublicspeakers.com
Books: - http://andy.chat/books
LinkedIn: - http://andy.chat/linkedin
Twitter: - http://andy.chat/twitter
Facebook: - http://andy.chat/facebook

Chapter 1

Eliminating Anxiety

1

Some Speakers Are So Confident

When you are attending meetings, have you ever paid careful attention to any of the speakers?

Maybe you have noticed how they always look so confident?

How they seem so relaxed before they deliver their presentation?

Continued

1

Some Speakers Are So Confident

Continued

How it is just us who gets nervous about having to speak in public?

In truth, every speaker feels some nerves in the lead up to delivering their presentation, even if they always look so calm, confident and competent.

It is entirely natural and normal for them to feel nervous as it is for you.

2

Seeing the Source

When faced with what can seem like a stressful situation such as speaking in public, it is easy to imagine how everything will go wrong.

Take a moment to think about what you are anxious about and the actual source of the stress you are feeling.

Create a list of anything that is causing you any anxiety.

3

Taking Action

Once you know the actual sources of the anxiety you are feeling about speaking, look to which ones you can take immediate action on to remove.

If you are unsure a meeting room is booked, call the booking team to confirm.

Will you need a projector for your presentation?

Speak with the AV team to establish a projector will be available on the day.

Continued

3

Taking Action

Continued

Concerned your colleagues may not remember to attend the meeting?

Send an email meeting reminder.

Taking action on the sources of anxiety that you can control and removing them will help you to feel more composed for your presentation.

4

Relieving the Anxiety

Aiming to have every word and gesture in your presentation perfected will increase the pressure felt as you worry about missing just a single word or action.

Rehearse your presentation so you know it, do not memorise it.

It will then be just like all those other stories you share every day where the words may change, but the core information stays consistent.

5

Staying Calm

One of the big worries for many of my clients in the lead-up to a meeting is that they may forget their words mid-way through their speech.

In the unlikely event this should ever happen, here is what you can do.

Pause, take a sip of water while calmly thinking of what you were saying.

Continued

5

Staying Calm

Continued

Casually look at your notes or even say to your audience with a smile 'now what was I saying...?'

Staying calm and composed is key as it allows you to think clearly and recall the next segment of your speech, while appearing confident and professional.

6

Seeking Support

First delivering your presentation to a small, supportive group of colleagues or friends will help to build your confidence.

The opportunity to rehearse in front of them, along with their support, encouragement and feedback will ensure you feel more confident for the meeting.

7

Presentation Posture

When feeling nervous, speakers will often slouch their shoulders and fold their arms.

This posture will make any feelings of nervousness seem far worse.

Before and during your presentation, aim to stand straight with your head up and back straight.

This posture will also enable you to breathe more deeply while appearing and feeling more confident.

8

Resisting Any Changes

The anxiety you may be feeling while waiting to speak at a meeting can cause you to start making changes to your presentation.

Often in the corporate world, I have seen speakers crossing out lines and writing in new ones minutes before they are due to speak.

Yep, I have done this too!

Fend off any thoughts of making any last-second changes, staying with the presentation you have prepared and practiced.

9

Notice Your Audience

While standing up in front of an audience, with everyone looking at us, we tend to focus on ourselves.

Worrying about being judged, our words, sentences and slides.

Redirecting your attention to your audience with help reduce any stress you are feeling.

As you look around the meeting, notice if they are interested in what you are presenting or appear to have any questions that they would like to ask you.

Chapter 2

Imperative Information

10

Discover Your Purpose

Every meeting at which you find yourself presenting will have a unique primary purpose.

When you have been invited to attend and speak at a meeting, ascertain the purpose of the meeting in advance of creating your presentation.

Knowing the purpose of the meeting will help you with the planning of your presentation.

11

One Question to Ask

As you are creating your presentation, there is one question that you will need to ask.

It is a question that you will need to ask yourself.

Ask what questions would be coming into your mind if you were sitting in the room and listening to the presentation.

Keep a list of the questions that come to mind as they can be incorporated into the final version of your presentation.

12

Timing Their Interest

What approach do you take when allotted a length of time to deliver a presentation at a meeting?

A standard approach taken when creating a presentation is for the speaker to think.

"I have 15 minutes, what can I tell them?"

A far more successful approach for you to take is: -

"I have 15 minutes, what would they like to know?"

13

Know Who Will Be There

As part of your preparation, find out the seniority of the people who have been invited to attend the meeting at which you are going to be speaking.

This information will allow you to create a speech that will be pitched at the level appropriate for their needs.

A presentation delivered to international directors of your company will be structured differently to one that is being given at a meeting with the Summer interns.

14

Assessing the Resources

The number attending the meeting will also have an influence on how your presentation is structured.

For example: -

- The number of handouts required.
- The design of any slides used.
- The time allocated for audience questions.

15

Advance Questions

Do you ever have an opportunity to speak at external meetings such as at a local networking group, community club or perhaps even at larger events?

When you have the chance to speak at external meetings, it will benefit you to know some details of the people who have previously presented at the meeting.

Once the invitation has been confirmed, some questions to consider asking the organiser are: -

Continued

15

Advance Questions

Continued

What did the organiser like about the speakers?

What subjects did the speakers cover?

What do they feel the other speakers could have done better?

This information will help you when creating your speech and ensure your success.

16

Who it is Really About

A presentation is never about you, your proposal, product or company.

People are sitting there and looking for solutions only to their problems.

Talk about the issues they face and how you will help to solve them.

They will then want to hear more from you.

Chapter 3

Investigating Ideas

17

Creativity of Your Hand

Do you ever find yourself looking forlornly at a blank document on your computer screen when it comes to the moment of creating your speech?

If this should ever happen to you, try writing your speech notes out by hand as the first stage of the drafting.

As writing by hand is more of a whole-body experience than typing, it provides the opportunity for you to think creatively, creating connections between all of your thoughts and ideas.

18

What is The Idea?

When starting to create your speech, there is one thing that you will need to settle on at the start of your preparation.

This is the single core idea that you want to convey to your audience.

What exactly is it that you would like everyone to know when you have concluded your speech?

What would you like them to be able to easily recall once they have returned to their desks?

Continued

18

What is The Idea?

Continued

Decide on that one core: -

>Tip
>
>Thing
>
>Thought

This single core idea will become the cornerstone of your speech structure, preparation and rehearsals.

19

Conveying Your Idea

Have you settled on your single core idea from the previous tip?

When starting to set out the structure your speech, list out each of the points required to convey the core idea of your speech to the audience.

At this stage add to the list any ideas that come to mind, even if they seem to be off topic.

Continued

19

Conveying Your Idea

Continued

While considering how to communicate the single core idea of your speech, think if it will help to include any: -

    Data

    Examples

    Illustrations

    Material

20

Trimming Your List

Have you completed your list as in the tip above?

Once you have completed your list, it is time to arrange each of the points into what you feel is a logical order to cover them.

Keep in mind the core idea of your speech as you review the list of your points.

Remove any of the points that will not directly contribute to helping the audience with their understanding of the core idea of your speech.

21

Building the Detail

With each point from the above tip created and arranged, now is the time to start adding in the details for each one.

Consider how each piece of information you have included can help your audience with their understanding of your speech and its single core idea.

If you find that any of the details are not directly contributing to helping your audience, they can be omitted from the speech.

22

Creating a Connection

If you are expecting an audience that is going to be hostile to your proposal, start your speech by creating a connection with them.

This could be achieved by highlighting your shared: -

- Background
- Interest
- Objectives
- Values

23

Exposing Concerns

Uncovering the reasons for any opposition to your proposal early in your presentation will provide an opportunity for you to address them.

If dealing with any opposition to a proposal is left until the end of the presentation or the closing question and answer session, it will be far harder for you to counteract any of their comments or questions with cogent reasoning.

Facing and dealing with any opposition as early as possible during your presentation is more likely to result in your proposal getting accepted.

24

Time to Browse

If it is on Google, it is true, or so some of the people attending your meeting may believe.

In advance of your speech, check to see what is currently being said on the internet about your subject matter.

It is totally fine to disagree with what has been written, especially if you believe it is incorrect or wrong.

By being aware of any other information allows you to decide if you will need to address it during your speech.

Chapter 4

Structuring Your Speech

25

Pique Their Interest

Will the title of your presentation be printed on the meeting agenda or announced by someone introducing you?

If so, give careful thought to what you select as the title of your presentation.

An imaginative title will pique everyone's interest and have them eager to hear your speech before you have said a single word.

Using a question as the title works well in company meetings.

26

Capturing Attention

The very first words of your speech are some of the most important.

Everyone attending the meeting will be deciding if they will listen to what you have to share with them while you are delivering the opening sentences.

If these first few sentences capture everyone's attention, they will become interested in your presentation.

27

Seeing the Sound

Onomatopoeic words are a super way to help your audience to picture the scenes that are being described in your presentation.

Onomatopoeic words sound like the ones they describe.

For example, the buzz of an office or the tick-tock of time.

See which words you can include in your next speech to help your audience see the scene or situation.

28

Advantages of Listening

Rather than starting your speech with those self-centred "I" focused phrases we will often hear from other speakers, instead share with everyone attending precisely what they will receive from listening to your presentation.

Briefly, outline to the audience the main advantages of what they will gain by listening to you.

29

Getting Personal

Sharing personal stories in a speech about your own experiences will immediately start to build the trust, confidence and connection people have with you.

As the audience sees your authenticity, conveying the central message or proposal of your speech will be more straightforward.

They will believe you understand them, their business, issues or concerns.

30

A Question to Contemplate

Stories that are added to a speech entirely to highlight your qualifications or show off how fantastic you consider yourself are of negligible value or interest to anyone.

Each of the personal stories added to your speech will be there to help your audience with their understanding of your message.

The question to have in your mind is how will this story help my audience?

31

Source of a Story

Stories that you choose to include in your speech may also come from other people. These may be: -

    Colleagues

    Clients

    Customers

Anyone who has experience of, or been affected by, the subject of your speech.

To save any awkward embarrassment, ask permission before including stories from other people.

32

Positive Endings

Whatever the source of the story included in your speech, the aim will be to leave the audience feeling positive and receptive.

To achieve this, you will want to have the story finish on a positive.

If it happens to be a story that does not have a 'happy ending', replace it with a story that does.

33

Discarding Details

While including stories in your speech helps with your audience's connection and comprehension, you will only need to add any details that are required to help your audience with their understanding.

Seek out and remove anything that diverts from the point you are making or are perhaps too personal to share in the meeting.

34

Paring the Points

Aiming to cover too many areas or points within the time allocated will result in your presentation being more arduous for your audience to comprehend.

Aim to cover an average of about one point for every 10 minutes you will be speaking.

This time scale will provide long enough for you to introduce the point, deliver a clear explanation and then a summary before moving on to the next area.

35

Aiding Recollection

To help your audience recall what you shared with them, you will find it helps to structure your speech into 3 distinct, clear sections or points.

As you progress through your speech, signpost each section as you progress through, creating a clear connection to each one.

When your audience later recalls one of the sections or points, the connections made will help them to recall the others that were covered in your speech.

36

Gathering the Points

If you have more than 3 points to cover in your presentation, place them together in groups.

For example, in one group you may cover the: -

    Pros

    Cons

    Recommendations

37

Captivating Comments

Creating a connection with the idea you are presenting to the audience is a central objective when speaking in public.

This connection can be created with the inclusion of thought-provoking comments and questions in your presentation.

These thought-provoking comments and questions will allow the attendees to go into their memories to imagine or recall how they did or would have felt.

Continued

37

Captivating Comments

Continued

After you have delivered your comment or question, briefly pause.

The pause and silence provide time for the attendees to think about what you have said to them.

Continue with your presentation once the time it would have taken you to have considered the comment or question has elapsed.

38

Confessing Your Concerns

If you feel there will be resistance to the proposal you are presenting, seek to address any concerns people are likely to have to the idea.

You will find it will help to address audience concerns early on in your presentation.

One way you can do this is to reveal some of the concerns you had when first hearing of the proposal yourself.

Continued

38

Confessing Your Concerns

Continued

You may explain early in the presentation how, when you first heard about the proposal, you were initially apprehensive and why you are now convinced of it and the benefits it will provide to them.

Sharing your initial apprehension will help people to be more open-minded to your proposal and hearing the details from you.

Chapter 5

Sharpening Your Speaking Skills

39

Audience Connections

You will sharpen your speaking skills by allowing time to rehearse the ideas and internalise the words of your speech.

The rehearsals will allow you to feel far more comfortable with the content.

Rather than delivering a lecture, your presentation will now become a conversation that connects with your audience and maintains their interest.

40

Making it Easy

Use rehearsals of your presentations as the time to discover if there are any words or phrases that trip you up.

These may be the simplest of words that you find are just not sounding or being pronounced as you have planned.

Presentation rehearsals are the perfect opportunity to swap out and replace these words with others that are easier for you to deliver.

41

Slowing the Speech

When your speech contains words which are easy for you to pronounce and deliver, it can be simple to speak at a faster pace than anticipated and rehearsed.

Speaking speeds will often increase when in front of an audience due to the anxiety that we can experience.

To help counteract this, rehearse your speech at a slightly slower pace than your average speaking speed.

42

Benefiting from Knowledge

There may be times when it will help to have your supportive colleagues sit in on the rehearsals of your presentation.

Your colleagues will be able to provide you with their feedback and assessment on how to make the presentation even better.

Continued

42

Benefiting from Knowledge

Continued

The feedback from your colleagues will be particularly useful to you when the presentation you are delivering is: -

   Technical

   Business specific

   Client focussed

43

Include it All

Seek to include in all of your rehearsals anything you may be using in your presentation. These can include:-

    Flip charts
    Slides
    Visual aids
    Props

By including these items in your rehearsals, it will help to ensure they each function as expected, help to illustrate the points you are making and that you are comfortable with how they all work and when to use them.

Chapter 6

PowerPoint Perfection

44

Looking the Best

The best fonts to use in your slides are those that are easy for your audience to read and look professional.

Script or handwritten type fonts may look great on your laptop screen but are harder to read on slides.

San serif fonts like Ariel and Helvetica are examples of fonts suitable for professional presentations.

45

Reducing the Files

The more pictures and graphics that are added to a presentation, the larger the file size of the final document will become.

The size of the file may be something you will need to consider if the presentation will be emailed, shared on a server or uploaded for a webinar.

PowerPoint and Keynote both have options that allow the file size to be reduced by either compressing the images or changing their resolution.

46

Explain and Expand

When every slide in a presentation contains paragraphs of text that the presenter reads out word for word, everyone attending the meeting will very quickly become bored.

A bored audience will quickly lose interest and simply stop listening to the presentation.

As we can all read faster than we speak, meeting attendees will have finished the slide before the speaker has completed reading out the first section.

Continued

46

Explain and Expand

Continued

People will soon wonder why they are sitting there as the slides could have been emailed to them.

Adding keywords rather than paragraphs to slides that you then explain and expand, will help with your audience's understanding and interest in your presentation.

47

Contacting the Speaker

You may find yourself on occasions presenting with slides at a meeting where the people attending have only just been introduced to you.

When presenting in these situations, take the opportunity to include a slide to share your contact details with the attendees.

Continued

47

Contacting the Speaker

Continued

The contact details you may like to include on your slide can include your: -

    Name
    Email address
    Phone number
    Website address
    LinkedIn profile address

Continued

47

Contacting the Speaker

Continued

Questions can come to mind long after the meeting at which you were speaking has concluded.

Providing your contact details during your presentation will help the meeting attendees to easily contact you if they have any follow up points to discuss or require any additional information.

48

Missing Mistakes

It is easy for us to miss our own mistakes with spelling or grammar.

To save showing any mistakes in public, invite a supportive colleague or friend to review your presentation slides.

Ask them to actively look for any errors and if they understood what it is that you are aiming to convey.

Completing the review in advance of your presentation will provide you with the time to update and revise the slides.

49

Timing Your Slides

The timing of when a presentation slide is displayed will have an impact on how much information your audience receives.

In meetings, you will often see speakers showing each slide before they mention the idea or point it supports.

You will find it more useful in helping your audience with their understanding to briefly introduce the point, then to show the slide that illustrates this information.

50

Showing Slides Online

When your presentation slides are going to be used for a Webinar, they can be uploaded directly to the provider's servers.

Many of the providers will flatten the file when the slides are uploaded.

This flattening process removes all the individual transitions so that they will appear together on a single slide.

Continued

50

Showing Slides Online

Continued

The resulting file will be similar to how you would view a presentation when it has been printed.

If the transitions are required, a workaround is to create an individual slide for each line of text or image.

The individual slides create the effect of having the transitions as you progress through the presentation.

51

Pressing the Right Buttons

Even the best-designed slides can sometimes become a distraction when left displayed while you are speaking.

The audience's attention can be directed from the slides and back to you by blanking the screen when the slides information is no longer required.

Most remote clickers have a button that will allow you to perform this action quickly.

Continued

51

Pressing the Right Buttons

Continued

On a keyboard, you can display a blank screen in PowerPoint by pressing W (white screen) or B (black screen).

If you are using Keynote, push the B key on your Mac keyboard.

Chapter 7

Presenting Your Presentation

52

Moving to Attention

As humans, we cannot resist looking at anything that is moving.

Even when we see something move in the corner of our eye, it catches our full attention.

This human trait can be utilised to help keep the meeting audience's attention on you and the presentation.

Continued

52

Moving to Attention

Continued

When you walk around the speaking area with intent and purpose, your audience will pay attention to you.

Everyone in the meeting will naturally be drawn to watch your movement and thereby to listen to the words of your presentation.

53

Adding Emphasis

Whatever the size of your speaking area, you are able to use it to add emphasis to the points covered in your presentation.

This emphasis can be achieved by standing at different spots in the speaking area as you deliver each of the key points.

Purposely walk to another part of the speaking area as you transition to the next point of your presentation.

Continued

53

Adding Emphasis

Continued

When you later refer back to the key points in your summary, gesture and look at the spot where you stood to deliver each point.

This will help your audience to recall the information you shared with them.

54

Backwards and Forwards

There is one part of the speaking area that will help you to emphasise essential or key points in your presentation.

This is the depth of the space available.

You can use the depth for helping reinforce any essential sections of your speech by taking a step or two forwards or backwards.

Continued

54

Backwards and Forwards

Continued

As an example, when it comes to the time when you are literally about to deliver a key point of your presentation, take one pace forward and towards your audience.

Deliver the point, then take a step back as everyone reflects on the point you have just made.

55

A Suitable Spot

An area often overlooked by speakers is the distance they stand from the front row of chairs or tables in the meeting room.

When a speaker is seen to be standing too far back from the audience, they can give the appearance of being nervous, detached or even aloof from everyone attending.

Continued

55

A Suitable Spot

Continued

On the other hand, a speaker who stands too close to the audience makes it harder for those at the front to see them as they need to keep looking up.

When you are aware of the two extremes, you will be able to find the most suitable spots to stand while delivering your speech.

56

Stepping Off the Stage

Larger meeting rooms or auditoriums may have a raised speaking area or stage installed for speakers to use.

While the stage will have been installed to help ensure everyone attending the meeting will be able to clearly see the speakers, you are able to leave it during your presentation.

Continued

56

Stepping Off the Stage

Continued

Stepping off the stage every now and then will help you to stand out from all the other speakers who are likely to remain on it.

As you leave the stage and walk in the area between the front row or even up the aisles, it will draw everyone's attention, helping to emphasise the point being made in your presentation.

Chapter 8

Confidently Answering Questions

57

Thinking of Your Own Questions

When you are delivering a presentation at a meeting, you will be perceived as the subject matter expert.

Knowing this allows you the opportunity to establish your credibility, knowledge and experience to everyone attending.

As part of your preparation, give thought to any questions you are likely to be asked during your presentation.

Continued

57

Thinking of Your Own Questions

Continued

The questions you think of will help to fill any gaps in your subject knowledge.

An approach that has worked for me is to think of what questions I would ask if sitting in the audience, listening to the presentation.

58

Who Will Be the Leader?

Sometimes you will find yourself delivering a presentation with another person like a colleague or supplier.

Decide in advance the arrangements for the Q&A session of your presentation.

Agree when to take questions and who will take the lead in answering them.

The presentation professionalism can start to quickly unravel if you talk over each other or even worse, disagree in public.

59

Express a Preference

During the opening segment of your presentation, share with the meeting your preference on when to ask any question they may have on the content covered.

If you express a preference for questions to be asked at the end of your presentation, be prepared for attendees to still ask questions as they occur to them.

This may be when they are unable to understand a particular point that has just been covered.

When prepared, you will be able to confidently answer questions before resuming your presentation.

60

Question to Ask

When it comes to the Q&A session, you will sometimes find people feel reluctant to be the first to ask a question.

You will feel more comfortable about facing this situation in your Q&A session by preparing a few questions of your own.

If there is silence when inviting questions from the meeting attendees, ask them one of your prepared questions.

Continued

60

Question to Ask

Continued

For example, if you have presented a proposal, you may ask: -

"How do you feel this proposal will affect your teams?"

Once you have asked the question, wait silently for people to start commenting on your question.

61

Choosing Your Question

An alternative approach to take when there is a reluctance to ask any questions is to give yourself one to answer.

You may say something like: -

"When I presented this proposal last week, I was asked…".

You will then proceed to respond to the question.

After you have answered the question, you will find people are more comfortable asking their own.

62

Valuing the Questions

When you are repeating the question to ensure everyone has heard it, ideally include the name of the person who asked.

You may do this by saying something like: -

'Maureen asked...'

Including the person's name will ensure the audience knows who it was that asked the question, while helping to make the person feel valued and their contribution appreciated.

63

Honesty is The Best Policy

Occasionally you will find that you do not understand a question, even after it has been repeated.

When this happens, be upfront with the person asking and request they help you by rephrasing the question.

The person asking will usually take this as an opportunity to expand their question, providing you with additional valuable information that will help with your answer.

64

Being Impolite

We were raised with the belief that it is polite to look at people when we are speaking to them.

This belief continues in meetings where speakers will often only look at the person who asked the question when answering.

When the answer is anything but brief, it can soon start to seem we are watching a private conversation.

We all like to feel included, so take the time to look around the room as this will keep everyone interested.

65

Serving Your Best

When a speaker is side-tracked to discuss an area of the subject they had not planned to cover by a member of the audience, the quality of their presentation can suffer.

The speaker will either need to rush later to stay on schedule, omit some of their content or run over time.

As these are not desirable outcomes for either the speaker or the audience, staying focussed on the prepared presentation will better serve everyone attending the meeting.

66

Achieving Focus

While we would like to give our full attention to every speaker when sitting in meetings, our focus does continuously vary.

When inviting a colleague whom you know will be able to answer the question, say their name first, in case their attention is focussed somewhere else.

After inviting your colleague to answer, repeat the question as they may have missed it being asked.

67

Encouraging Participation

A member of the audience may ask a question or make a point that you feel is incorrect during your presentation.

It will help you to retain audience participation if your reply does not start with "no, that is wrong…".

This type of response can prompt the person asking to enter into a debate with you or leave them feeling embarrassed.

Continued

67

Encouraging Participation

Continued

Other people in the meeting will pick up on this, so may avoid speaking up to avoid getting into the same situation.

Look for less direct ways to start your reply like "my feeling is…", "the general view is…", or "other people feel…", then share your reasons.

This will encourage other people to participate in your presentation.

Chapter 9

Visual Communication

68

Creating a Natural Connection

When you are able to look naturally around the meeting room while delivering your speech, the connection you make with each of the attendees will help you to feel more relaxed and confident.

Can you imagine how it will feel to see the interest and engagement of your colleagues as you are speaking?

Continued

68

Creating a Natural Connection

Continued

The way to make eye contact naturally is to look at someone as you deliver a single sentence.

As you finish the sentence, slowly move your focus to someone else in another part of the room.

Repeat the action for each sentence, gradually covering the entire room.

69

Naturally Gesturing

While delivering your presentation, you will instinctively be making gestures with your body. These gestures will most often be focussed on your hands, arms and face.

Each of the gestures made in your presentation will have more of an effect when they are natural and in the moment rather than having been rigorously rehearsed.

There is an essential reason for this.

Continued

69

Naturally Gesturing

Continued

When a gesture has been created and rehearsed, it will be performed on the cue of a specific word.

This leads the gesture appearing to be out of sync with the words you are delivering, with a time lag between what your audience hears and then sees with the gesture.

When your gestures are made without conscious thought, they will come across as instinctive and natural.

70

Showing Your Hand

You will create a more positive impression on your audience when your hands stay on show and visible during your presentation.

The opposite occurs when a speaker continually hides their hands in trouser pockets or behind their back.

When a speaker is hiding their hands, people will start to believe they have something to hide, so are less likely to believe what they are saying.

71

Controlling Your Confidence

A speech is not over when you stop speaking.

Maintain your confidence and professionalism as your speech concludes and you leave the speaking area.

Speakers will sometimes walk off looking sullen, beaten or even elated, all of which are seen by the audience.

When you walk off looking confident, it will help the audience to maintain their trust in you.

Chapter 10

Recording and Reviewing

72

Finding Your Favourites

We all have our favourite words we use in our conversations.

When you record and view the recordings of your past presentations, listen for any word that you are repeatedly using as this will help you to seek out alternatives.

For example, when speakers say 'that is a good point...', they could instead say it is a 'fascinating', 'exciting' or 'superb' point.

73

Repetitive Gestures

Aim to watch the recordings of your speeches with the sound turned off and at double speed or faster.

This will help you to see any unconscious, repetitive gestures or actions that you are making while presenting.

Once you are aware of any repetitive gestures or movements, you will be able to look at growing this area of your presentation skills.

74

Seeing a Straight Stance

Notice how you stand while speaking when watching the recordings of your presentations.

Maybe you are standing straight and looking confident, or perhaps slightly slouched and appearing a little nervous?

When you start your speech by having adopted the straight stance we covered earlier, you will begin to feel more confident throughout your speech.

Chapter 11

Success Planning

75

Arranging Your Resources

Will people be joining the meeting to listen to your presentation from another office?

If you have people joining your meeting remotely from another location, aim to have all the resources you plan to show or distribute in your presentation made available to them in advance.

These resources may be provided to attendees by email or with a link to a shared area that they can easily access.

76

Planning a Positive Impression

When you are being formally introduced at the meeting at which you are speaking, take time to prepare a written introduction.

Creating this document is a principal part of your preparation as it can immediately affect how the people attending the meeting will perceive you.

What is it you would like the attendees to know about you and your subject?

Continued

76

Planning a Positive Impression

Continued

It will be worth printing a couple of copies of your introduction and taking it along to the meeting with you, even if you have emailed the information in advance to the organiser.

In meetings, when people have a lot on their minds with different documents and speakers, they can easily misplace papers.

77

Dressing to Impress

When dressing for the meeting, you will naturally be keen to look your very best.

Consider any jewellery you are planning to wear for the speech and whether it will be in any way distracting for your audience.

For example, your favourite earrings may look stunning, but if they reflect the room lighting like a lighthouse, they are best left at home.

78

Contrasting Clothes

When presenting at a larger event in an auditorium, there is likely to be a raised area or stage for the speakers.

If you are going to be delivering your speech in an auditorium, find out in advance the colour of the backdrop and take this into consideration when choosing your clothes.

If the colour of your clothes happens to match the backdrop, it will be harder for people to see you.

79

Awareness of Announcements

Aim to be aware of what is on the minds of the people you are presenting to before you get up to speak.

Will a previous speaker have delivered some good or bad news that everyone will be thinking about while you are speaking?

By understanding the people attending the meeting and how they are going to be feeling, you will be able to adapt your energy and opening for them.

80

Preparing for Probability

The best-laid plans can be affected by office issues, calls and clients.

If people are delayed, it may change the meeting timing and therefore cause changes to the agenda.

Be prepared for all eventualities, ensuring you arrive on time in case you now need to speak earlier than initially scheduled.

Chapter 12

Showing Up and Stepping Up

81

Need to Know?

When you arrive at the meeting at which you are speaking, ask the manager or organiser if there is anything they would like you to know.

This simple, open question can reveal valuable information such as who will be attending, challenges with the room set-up, even any last-minute changes to the meeting agenda.

82

Every Little Thing Matters

If you sent an advance copy of your presentation to the meeting organiser, take a look at it before the meeting starts.

Check to see that: -

>Your presentation has been copied to the computer.

>The correct version has been opened.

>Each of the slides changes as planned when you click through them.

>Any animations display correctly.

83

Checking the Connection

Will you have anyone listening to your next presentation on a conference call or a video connection?

To avoid any last-minute disruption, check to see if any of the following are required and can be available and set-up ready before you start your speech: -

    Conference phone

    Microphone

    Camera

84

Amplified for Audio

If you are going to be using a microphone for your speech, allow time to test it works in advance of the meeting starting.

When supplied with a hand-held microphone, ask for advice on the best way to hold it and how far from your mouth to help provide the best reception.

Check if a member of the audio-visual team will turn it on and off or will you need to do so just before you begin to speak.

85

Sidestep the Buzz

When wearing a microphone and carrying out the tests mentioned in the previous tip, look to see if there are any parts of the speaking area that you may need to avoid due to a risk that they will create that high-pitched feedback sound we all dislike.

Knowing where to avoid standing will save any interruptions to the flow if your speech.

86

Promptly Preparing

As part of your preparation when arriving early in the meeting room, place anything that is required for your presentation in the speaking area such as: -

Pens
Papers
Props
Presentation clicker

This preparation will allow you to confidently walk to the front of the room with your hands empty, helping you to appear confident, prepared and professional.

87

Seeing the Speaker

One of the reasons lighting levels can be set low in auditoriums is to help attendees to see the slides being shown.

You are the presentation, rather than the slides which are a 'visual aid'.

Ask for the lighting levels to be set at the level that ensures all the meeting attendees can clearly see you.

88

Eradicating Diversions

While in the meeting room and waiting to deliver your presentation, remove from your trouser and jacket pockets anything that is noisy such as keys or loose change.

The sounds they make jangling can cause a disturbance and distraction to the meeting attendees as they listen to your presentation.

89

Protruding Pockets

While removing the keys or loose change from your pockets, also take out anything that is bulging such as wallets or phones before delivering your presentation.

Removing these items will save the audience having to wonder what it is that is sticking out of your pocket while you are speaking.

90

Your Crucial Sentences

When speaking at larger or more structured meetings where you are a guest, there will usually be someone to introduce you.

They are the person who will deliver the prepared introduction we covered earlier in this book.

A standard way you will see other speakers start their speech is to repeat what their introducer has just said about them.

Continued

90

Your Crucial Sentences

Continued

This is such a waste of those crucial first few sentences of their speech.

You will help the success of your speech by using this time to say something that will grab everyone's focus and attention, ensuring they want to listen to your presentation.

Chapter 13

Presentation Perfection

91

Sticking to It

When you have a prepared opening for your speech, stick to it!

When feeling under stress, there can be a temptation to change the first couple of sentences.

Deciding to stick with them will save you from being distracted by anything else that may have just happened or been said by another speaker.

92

Source of Stress

Speaking at a meeting with other presenters can be an added source of stress.

This additional stress comes from the concern that the other speakers may look more confident and self-assured.

Rather than thinking about the other speakers, focussing on the presentation and serving the audience will help you to feel more confident.

93

Talking to the Wall

As you arrive in the speaking area, resist the urge to start speaking immediately.

Speakers feeling the stress of the moment can sometimes begin their speech even before they have been able to turn around to face the audience.

Speaking before facing the audience results in the prepared opening line of the speech being unheard by most of the people attending the meeting.

94

Short Summary

The attention levels of the people listening to your presentation will naturally vary while you are speaking.

To help meeting attendees who may have missed part of your presentation with their understanding of the subject, before moving on to the next area, include a summary of all the points you have just covered.

Including regular short summaries will help to ensure everyone has the same level of subject comprehension as you progress through your presentation.

95

Seeing the Signs

There are some common signs that could indicate a level of concern, confusion or doubt that you may see on the faces of your audience.

These signs include: -

    Frowning

    Scratching their head

    Appearing slightly agitated

    Raising one eyebrow higher than the other

96

Releasing Their Concerns

If you see apparent disagreement from anyone in the meeting to a proposal you are presenting, address it as soon as possible.

If a difference of opinion is left unaddressed, the audience members will hold onto it, waiting for the chance to share their opinion.

Continued

96

Releasing Their Concerns

Continued

While waiting, they will either ignore the rest of your speech or possibly wait until later and challenge you in the Q&A part of the meeting when there is less time for you to address their points of concern.

Once the point has been discussed and resolved, briefly recap your last point before resuming your presentation.

97

Private Conversation

There may be times when you are midway through your presentation that you find a couple of people attending the meeting start holding a quiet, private conversation.

What should you do when in this situation?

If the conversation is not disrupting the meeting and is short, there is no need to say or do anything as their attention will soon return back to you.

98

Keeping Your Credibility

Ad-libbing during a speech that you have prepared and practiced is where the chance of a quip or comment could creep in and cause offence.

Sidestep any comments from your audience that can lead you into saying something inappropriate.

A single comment that upsets just one person is all it takes to damage your credibility.

99

Pausing for Confidence

There are times where you will find it invaluable to pause for a couple of seconds while delivering your presentation. These times may be: -

> At the very start of your speech while making eye contact with your audience.
>
> Just before or after you have made an important point.
>
> Just before or after you have shared something that you would like the audience to reflect on.
>
> Immediately after you have delivered the final words of your speech.

Continued

99

Pausing for Confidence

Continued

While pausing and standing in silence at the front of the room for a couple of seconds may seem scary as you think about it, doing so will help you.

As you take the time to pause, it provides you with the opportunity to breathe and think of your next point, helping to build your confidence.

100

Sharing the Sentiment

Every audience feels and feeds off the energy of the speaker.

When you deliver your presentation with conviction, passion and enthusiasm, it will be felt by everyone listening.

If you are saying something is exciting, projecting this belief will help your audience to feel the excitement you are describing to them.

101

Significant Slip?

While delivering your presentation, you may miss out a word or sentence that you had intended to say.

Does this omission affect the purpose or message of your presentation?

Will the audience be affected in any way?

The chances are that the oversight will have absolutely no effect, so let it pass and remain focused on serving your audience.

ABOUT ANDY O'SULLIVAN

How to achieve success in the business world

In his books, workshops and seminars, Andy teaches professionals how to dramatically increase their rise up the corporate career ladder and grow their business by creating and presenting presentations that inspire, impress and ensure they are the obvious choice.

Andy enjoyed a successful corporate career that saw him working for many of the leading financial institutions and international banks.

It was while working in the corporate world that Andy recognised the need to develop his own public speaking and presentation skills.

A long and, at times, painful journey that led him to develop the renowned Corporate Confidence System™.

The Corporate Confidence System™ utilises all of Andy's knowledge and extensive experience from the real world, so professionals are now able to swiftly create speeches that connect with clients, colleagues and even the CEO.

The incredible success of the Corporate Confidence System™ and constant demand by entrepreneurs and startup founders for Andy to share his extensive experience with them, led to the development of the now acclaimed Startup Success System™.

About Andy O'Sullivan

A system that ensures entrepreneurs and startup founders are able to create pitches that will impress their important investors and buyers, winning them that crucial investment or order.

The commitment Andy has continually shown in helping people to learn effective public speaking and presentation skills has been recognised by all the international awards and accolades he has received.

Andy is the founder of the Academy of Public Speakers, a leading provider of public speaking and presentation skills training.

You can contact Andy directly at: -

Andy@academyofpublicspeakers.com
www.academyofpublicspeakers.com
LinkedIn: - http://andy.chat/linkedin
Twitter: - http://andy.chat/Twitter
Facebook: - http://andy.chat/facebook
Books: - http://andy.chat/books

Acknowledgments

I will never be able to express enough thanks to my Mum for her never-ending love and support. Standing by me and always being there throughout the bad times as well as the good.

To my sister Maureen for her love, patience and fantastic assistance with all of my books.

To my sister Teresa for those early lessons in English.

To my brother Peter for being my willing and original chauffeur.

Thanks to Tanvir Arafat for his incredible positivity, awesome support, amazing ideas and cherished friendship.

To Hien Vo for the endless extent of his encouragement and friendship which is forever valued.

Thanks to Keny Castro-Moreno for his willing and wonderful support that he has provided with my recent books.

To Naynesh Patel for always being there and willing to give me a helping hand whenever I asked and even when I didn't.

Thanks to Rob Hemsley for his ardent assistance with the PR machine he very kindly created and managed.

Thanks to Shyam Gupta for seeing the potential in me and giving up his time to help at my first series of events.

Acknowledgments

Thanks to Michael for working so hard to give us all that he possibly could.

To Ralph C. Smedley without whom my journey of self-development and growth would have been so much longer and harder.

A final word of gratitude to all those who have guided and supported me during my long and at times painful journey.

References

Mail Online (2018). Scientists reveal the harder you chew gum, the greater the relief. [online] Available at: http://www.dailymail.co.uk/health/article-3241135/Gum-keeps-Jose-ball-Scientists-reveal-harder-chew-greater-relief.html. Web. 3 Feb. 2018

Rodionova, Zlata. "The 12 Words To Say In An Interview That Can Land (Or Lose) You The Job". The Independent. N.p., 2016. Web. 1 Apr. 2016.

"Serial Position Effect ". Indiana.edu. N.p., 2016. Web. 1 Apr. 2016.

"Presentation - Definition Of Presentation In English From The Oxford Dictionary". Oxforddictionaries.com. N.p., 2016. Web. 1 Apr. 2016.

"Pitch - Definition Of Pitch In English From The Oxford Dictionary". Oxforddictionaries.com. N.p., 2016. Web. 1 Apr. 2016.

"7 Shocking Health Statistics". Realbuzz 4. N.p., 2012. Web. 1 Apr. 2016.

Bibliography

Avery, Matt. Successful Public Speaking In A Week. London: Teach Yourself, 2013. Print.

Beebe, Steven, and Beebe, Susan. Public Speaking, An Audience-Centered Approach. Mass.: Pearson, 2013. Print

Eldin, Peter et al. Speechmakers' Bible. London: Cassell Illustrated, 2006. Print.

Fripp, Patricia and LaCroix. Create Your Keynote By Next Week. USA: DVD.

Godefroy, Christian H, Stephanie Barrat-Godefroy, and Christian Godefroy. Confident Public Speaking. London: Piatkus, 1998. Print.

Jeffreys, Michael. Success Secrets Of The Motivational Superstars. Rocklin, CA: Prima Pub., 1996. Print.

Ledden, Emma. The Presentation Book. Harlow: Pearson, 2013. Print.

Linver, Sandy, and Jim Mengert. Speak And Get Results. New York: Simon & Schuster, 1994. Print.

Lucas, Stephen. The Art Of Public Speaking. Boston: McGraw-Hill Higher Education, 2009. Print.

Mueck, Florian. The Seven Minute Star. [North Charleston, S.C.]: [Createspace], 2010. Print.

Valentine, Craig, and Mitch Meyerson. World Class Speaking In Action. New York: Morgan James, 2015 Print.

Bibliography

Weissman, Jerry, and Jerry Weissman. Successful Presentation Strategies. Upper Saddle, New Jersey: FT Press, 2013. Print.

Yazbeck, Joe. No Fear Speaking. Odessa, FL: Paradies Publishing Co., 2014. Print.

Public Speaking Success

101 Proven Steps to Successful Speeches, Pitches & Presentations

Andy O'Sullivan

www.ingramcontent.com/pod-product-compliance
Lightning Source LLC
Chambersburg PA
CBHW052252220526
45471CB00001B/297